Bethy's Mum is in Prison

Lorna Brookes and
Emily Livsey

Illustrated by Aoife J O'Dwyer

≋ WATERSIDE PRESS

From the My Parent in Prison Series

Bethy lives with her Nan and her cat Rudy.

Bethy's Mum is in prison.

Today is a school day.

Bethy and her Nan are walking to school practicing spellings.

Bethy has a spelling test today.

Bethy is really good at spelling.

After school Bethy's Nan is cooking dinner.

Bethy is watching TV with her cat Rudy.

Bethy looks sad.

Nan asks Bethy, *"What's wrong?"*

Bethy says, *"Today we were making Mother's Day cards in school."*

"*That's hard*", says Nan.

Bethy says *"A girl in my class asked me why I don't live with my Mum. I didn't know what to say".*

Nan says, *"Yes that's hard too. Perhaps you could say, I don't want to talk about it?"*

Nan gives Bethy a big hug.

Bethy looks forward to visiting her Mum in prison. She ticks off the days on a big calendar in the kitchen.

Bethy's school understands that visits are very important to Bethy and allows Bethy to take time off school to go and see Mum when she needs to.

On visiting day, Bethy and Nan
have to take two buses.

It takes a long time to get to the visit.

Bethy takes a bag full of things to
do and play with on the bus.

In the visit Bethy tells Mum that she got full marks in her spelling test.

"I'm so proud of you", says Mum.

Bethy does not like the end of the visits because saying goodbye is really hard.

She gives Mum a big hug.

"Don't be sad", says Mum. *"I'll see you soon and I will talk to you on the phone".*

In school, Bethy's sees another girl, Abbie crying. Abbie's best friend has moved to another school and Abbie misses her.

"We can play together if you like?" says Bethy.

"Okay" says Abbie.

Bethy and Abbie play with the stuffed animals together.

Abbie asks *"Bethy, why don't you live with your Mum?"*

"I don't want to talk about that", says Bethy.

"But I still have a Mum even though we don't live together right now. We talk on the phone, and I visit her. When I miss her, I look at pictures of my Mum and me, and I write her letters or draw her pictures. You could send your friend a card in the post if you miss her?"

"That's a good idea" says Abbie.

"Let's make cards together".

Abbie and Bethy have fun making cards.
They use lots of stickers and colours.

The next day in school assembly, some children are getting awards. Bethy is called to the stage. Bethy feels very excited to hear her name called.

Bethy's teacher says, *"This week Bethy is Star of the Week, for being so kind and such a good friend to others".*

The teacher gives Bethy a certificate and a big gold star. All the children clap loudly. Abbie claps the loudest of all.

Bethy feels very happy.

"I cant wait to tell Mum on the phone tonight" she thinks to herself.

Bethy knows her Mum is going to be so proud of her and she smiles the biggest of smiles.

We are a service that supports children and young people who have a parent or family member in prison. We also support children and young people before a parent has gone to prison if it is likely they will go into custody, and after a parent has been released.

We were established in 2017 under the name 'MyTime' before changing our name to Time-Matters. We also provide training for organizations who wish to set up a similar service in their own geographical area.

Where are we?

We are based on Merseyside in the UK, but we welcome children from any locality. We are not affiliated to any particular prison; rather our support is community-based. Support takes place face-to-face in various venues including community centres, youth clubs, schools, and online.

What do we do?

Peer Support Groups: Therapeutic support groups enable children and young people to discuss their feelings and consider coping strategies with trained practitioners and other young people who share their experience. Normally there are around 5–15 children in a group. Groups might be face-to-face or online. We address difficult issues, but we also have fun. We are child and youth centred. We believe our groups help build resilience in children and young people.

1:1 Mentoring: Children and young people are able to access bespoke 1:1 mentoring delivered by trained volunteers. We know that every child is different and every experience of having a parent or family member in prison is different. These sessions are therefore really helpful for children to explore their feelings, in a more private setting, with one mentor who takes the time to get to know their personality, interests and particular challenges they might want help with.

Children as Changemakers: We see the children and young people who attend our service as experts of their own experience. We provide them with the opportunity to be leaders and